NEW YORK

THEN AND NOW®
People and Places

NEW YORK
CITY AND STATE

THEN AND NOW®
People and Places

First published in the United Kingdom in 2013 by
PAVILION BOOKS
10 Southcombe Street, London W14 0RA
An imprint of Anova Books Company Ltd

ISBN: 978-1-86205-995-5

A CIP catalogue record for this book is available from the British Library.

Printed by 1010 Printing International Limited, China.

10 9 8 7 6 5 4 3 2 1

The Statue of Liberty, 1952

The Statue of Liberty, 1905

Arriving at Ellis Island, c. 1910

Ellis Island, c. 1915

Ellis Island, c. 1910

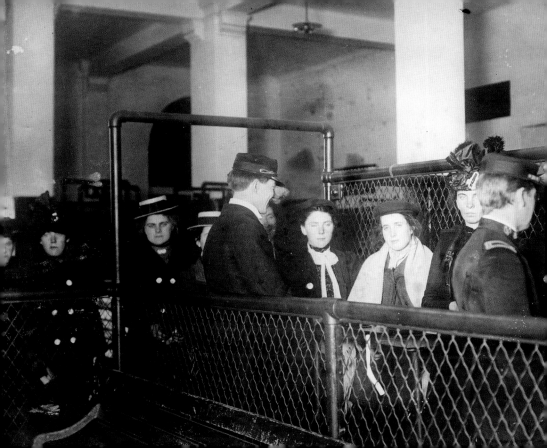

Ellis Island, c. 1910

Battery Park, c. 1905

Broadway and Battery Place from Bowling Green, 1908

Custom House, Bowling Green, 1908

New York Stock Exchange, Broad Street, c. 1910

South Street Seaport, c. 1890

World Trade Center, 1999

World Trade Center, 1999

Transportation and Woolworth Buildings, 1999 (left), 1939 (right)

Brooklyn Bridge, 1982

Brooklyn Bridge, 1904

Brooklyn Bridge, 1999

Brooklyn Bridge from Front Street, 1982

City Hall, 1905

City Hall Subway Station, c. 1905

50

SAYVILLE LIBRARY

Manhattan Municipal Building, 1914

St Paul's Chapel, c. 1890

Washington Market at Warren and Greenwich Streets, c. 1912

P.S. 234, The Independence School

Pell Street, Chinatown, c. 1910

Mott Street, Chinatown, c. 1910

Mott Street, Chinatown, 1965

Manhattan Bridge under construction, 1909

65

Manhattan Bridge

67

Mulberry Street, Little Italy, c. 1900

Broadway at Grand Street, 1860

Third Avenue and Ninth Street, 1910

Run on German Bank, 147 Fourth Avenue, 1914

Lafayette Street, 1914

Grace Church, 1910

106 Macdougal Street, 1914

Seventh Avenue at Christopher Street, 1970

Bleeker Street from Thompson Street, 1914

Washington Arch, Washington Square Park, 1900

Washington Arch, Washington Square Park, c. 1955

White Horse Tavern, Hudson and Eleventh Streets, 1961

East 23rd at Park Avenue, c. 1905

SEEING
NEW YORK

SEEING
NEW YORK

"SEEING NEW YORK"

STARTS FROM FLAT IRON BUILDING
TELEPHONE CONNECTION.

Sightseeing bus in front of Flatiron Building, c. 1910

Flatiron Building, c. 1905

Flatiron Building from Madison Square Park, c. 1905

Metropolitan Life Building, under construction (1909) and completed (1911)

Metropolitan Life Building from Madison Avenue, c. 1910

Clerks on the roof of the Metropolitan Life Building, c. 1915

Union Square, c. 1905

A shoe-shine boy in Union Square, 1913

Union Square, 1913

Sixth Avenue and 14th Street, 1910

Hotel Chelsea, West 23rd Street, c. 1955

Messenger boys at Sixth Avenue and 32nd Street, 1916

INTRODUCED AT "THE NEW YORK TIMES"
INTRODUCED AT "GQ"
INTRODUCED AT "ESQUIRE"
INTRODUCED AT "PIX 11 MORNING NEWS"

Macy's, 1939 (left) and c. 1910 (right)

Macy's, 1908

Herald Square, c. 1910

Herald Square

Broadway & 33rd Street, Horace Greeley Monument, New York City. 25925

The Waldorf-Astoria, c. 1900

Empire State Building, 1930

154

Empire State Building, c. 1935

View from the Empire State Building, 1932

View from the Empire State Building, 1933

Chrysler Building under construction, 1929

Chrysler Building from Second Avenue, c. 1930

163

Chrysler Building, 1930

Chrysler Building from 42nd Street, c. 1945

Grand Central Station under construction, 1912

Grand Central Station, c. 1915

Grand Central Station, 1913

Grand Central Station, 1913

TO LOWER LEVEL

TO PARCEL ROOM

Grand Central Station, 1929

Grand Central Station, 1913

Main waiting room, Grand Central Station, 1913

United Nations Headquarters, 1966

East River looking north toward Queensboro Bridge, 1938

Park Avenue at 54th Street, 1961

189

St. Patrick's Cathedral, c. 1905

St. Patrick's Cathedral, c. 1905

194

Fifth Avenue at East 50th Street, c. 1960

Bryant Park, c. 1937

City experiment in gardening, Bryant Park, 1918

Bryant Park

New York Public Library, c. 1910

New York Public Library, c. 1910

New York Public Library and Fifth Avenue, 1913

New York Public Library, c. 1910

Port Authority Bus Terminal, c. 1960

Rockefeller Center, 1943

Broadway at 44th Street, 1943

218

Watching the news on the Times Building, 1944

221

Broadway and Seventh Avenue at 47th Street

223

Broadway at 49th Street, 1958

Times Square, 1943 (left) and 1930 (right)

Times Square, 1957

Times Square, 1969 (left) and 1955 (right)

Broadway from the Times Building, c. 1915

West 52nd Street, 1948

Radio City Music Hall, c. 1960

Carnegie Hall, c. 1940

Plaza Hotel, c. 1910

Maine Monument, Columbus Circle, 1921

Central Park at 59th Street, 1901

Central Park Lake, c. 1915

Central Park Lake, c. 1905

Belvedere Castle, Central Park, c. 1900

Bow Bridge, Central Park, c. 1900

Bow Bridge, Central Park, 1984

Bethesda Terrace and Fountain, Central Park

The Metropolitan Museum, 1914

Statuary Hall (left) and Jade Room (right), The Metropolitan Museum, 1905

Solomon R. Guggenheim Museum under construction, 1957

Lincoln Center, c. 1965

Lincoln Center, c. 1965

Lincoln Center, c. 1965

Lincoln Center, c. 1965

The Dakota Building from Central Park, c. 1890

12 11 CENTRAL SAVINGS BANK

Cathedral of St. John the Divine, 1913

Columbia University Library, 1901

George Washington Bridge, 1930

TO THE DEFENDERS OF THE UNION 1861 1865

Memorial Arch from Prospect Park, Brooklyn, c. 1900

Atlantic Avenue Station, Brooklyn, c. 1915

Coney Island, Brooklyn, c. 1900

Coney Island, Brooklyn, c. 1910 (left) and 1905 (right)

Coney Island, Brooklyn, c. 1905

Parachute Jump from Boardwalk, Coney Island, Brooklyn, c. 1960

JetBlue Terminal, JFK Airport, Queens

The Unisphere, Flushing Meadows, Queens, 1965

Botanical Gardens Museum, Bronx Park, The Bronx, 1906

New York State Capitol, Albany, c. 1913

Hawk Street Viaduct and New York State Capitol, Albany, c. 1910

State Street, Albany, c. 1904

Union Station, Albany, c. 1910

Broadway, Saratoga Springs, c. 1910

Broadway, Saratoga Springs, c. 1910

American and Adelphi Hotels, Saratoga Springs, c. 1910

The First Sagamore Hotel, Green Island, Lake George, 1907

The First Sagamore Hotel, Green Island, Lake George, 1907

The First Sagamore Hotel, Green Island, Lake George, 1907

The First Sagamore Hotel, Green Island, Lake George, 1907

The First Sagamore Hotel, Green Island, Lake George, 1907

Sagamore Hotel (rebuilt after 1914 fire), Green Island, Lake George

Morrill Hall and McGraw Tower, Cornell University, Ithaca, c. 1900

CARS STOP HERE

Soldiers' and Sailors' Monument, Lafayette Square, Buffalo, c. 1913

Darwin D. Martin House, Buffalo, 1973

Ellicott Square Building, Buffalo, 1900

American Falls, Niagara Falls, c. 1910

American Falls from Prospect Point, Niagara Falls, c. 1910

Acknowledgments

All "now" photographs are by David Watts, except for the following:
Paulm27: 13. Jean-Christophe Benoist: 17. Momos: 49. John-Paul
Palescandolo: 51. Chensiyuan: 59. Jim Henderson: 133. Jon Nool: 146–147.
Norbert Nagel: 159. Alamy: 222–223. David Shankbone: 295. Daniel Case:
297. Gryffindor: 301. Dmadeo: 343.

All "then" photographs are courtesy the Library of Congress, except for the
following: Anova Image Library: 30, 38, 44, 94, 100, 118, 149, 150, 154, 156,
162, 198, 212, 232, 233, 242, 286, 288, 290, 292, 332, 334, 336, 338. New
York Historical Society: 54, 76, 312. Corbis: 64, 134, 185, 188–189. NYC
Municipal Archives: 65, 163, 176, 244. NYC Vintage Images: 88, 266, 268,
295. André Robé: 166, 230, 231. Getty Images: 192, 196–197, 230. Rex
Features: 220–221. Alamy: 224–225.

Cover: Broadway and Seventh Avenue at 47th Street, 1959 (Rex Features).
Page 2: New York City street scene by Arthur Rothstein, 1941 (Library of
Congress).

Researched, compiled and edited by David Salmo of Anova Books.